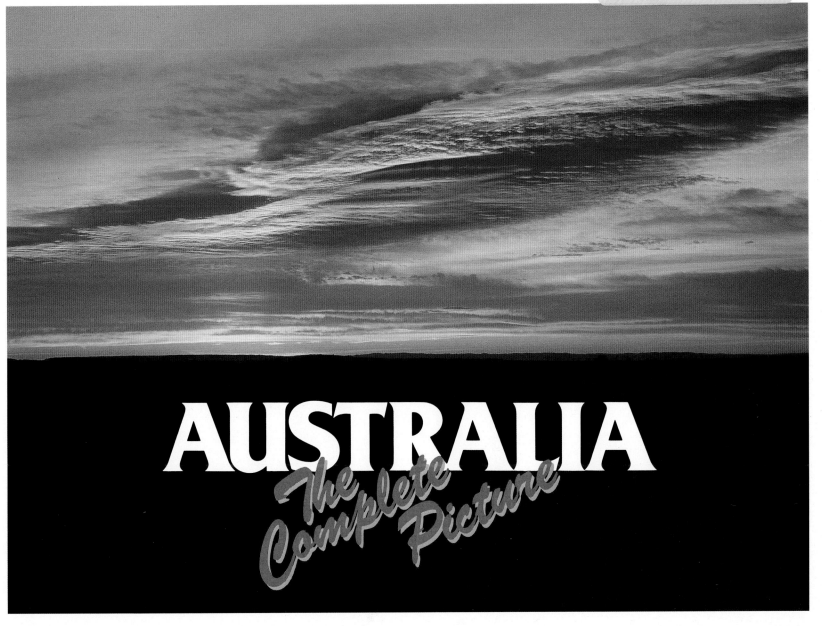

AUSTRALIA
The Complete Picture

PHOTOGRAPHY BY GARY LEWIS

Copyright© 1989
Peter Antill-Rose
& Associates

PA·R

Castle Hill
New South Wales 2154
Australia

AUSTRALIA
The Complete Picture

PHOTOGRAPHY BY GARY LEWIS

Palm Valley, Northern Territory

Contents

Introduction

Australians are often amused by the images some foreigners have of Australia, and bemused by the slick advertising imagery of the emerging tourist industry. But if pressed to say what Australia is really like, many of these same Australians would find themselves trotting out variations on the tired old cliches about sunshine, kangaroos, drovers and Ayers Rock. What is Australia really like? Well...

There are no easy answers. Australia is an ancient land, its mountain ranges have been ground away to rough hills, its creatures are bizarre left-overs from an earlier age; and yet it is also a new land, its cities barely one or two hundred years old, its writers, artists and musicians only now finding a truly Australian voice. It is a land of dazzling desiccating sunlight, of torrential monsoonal rain, of alpine blizzards, of soft misty mornings, and crisp autumn afternoons. If the Australian bush is the drab olive of eucalypts, it is also the icy aqua of young bluegum leaves, the warm yellow of wattle blossom in winter, the multicoloured carpet of everlastings on the red desert sand after rain, the yellows, creams, whites, pinks and scarlets of honey-scented gum blossom, and the endless variety of wildflowers in spring.

The Australian economy 'rides on the sheep's back', and yet Australian business people, technicians, researchers, and professionals are responsible for some of the greatest technological, medical and scientific advances, and head some of the world's big businesses. In the city, a life begins in a 'test-tube', aided by the very latest in medical technology; on a distant station, a shearer hauls a sheep out of the pen to shear it in much the same way as a shearer of last century.

This land is desert, it is endless kilometres of sandy surf beaches, it is pockets of precious rainforest, rolling green pasture, alpine heathlands, city parks, hectares of suburbs, and towering

skyscrapers. It is a country that has produced world-class sports women and men, a string of internationally acclaimed sopranos, film star Paul 'Mick Dundee' Hogan, and Nobel-Prize-winning author Patrick White.

The two best-known silhouettes in the country are probably Ayers Rock and the Sydney Opera House. This country stops work for a horse race, and claims its worst military disaster as a national triumph of the spirit.

And the people? Go back a few generations and you would find the ancestors of today's Australians scattered all over the world, in English prisons, on poor Scottish or Irish farms, in a Polish ghetto, on a Californian goldfield, or the bustling streets of Saigon. Only the Aboriginals can trace an unbroken line back 40 000 years in this country. Australia is a multicultural nation, and yet after one or two generations of native-born children, there is something distinctly Australian about them. We are a nation of city-dwellers that dreams of the bush.

Contradictory, confusing, multi-faceted – that's Australia. This book throws a few more images into the melting pot and allows you to choose your own Australia.

Ancient aboriginal paintings, Alice Springs, Northern Territory

History and Antiquity

At Lake Mungo in north-eastern Victoria, archaeological finds have established the presence of human beings in Australia some 40 000 years ago. Two human burials, one of a young woman and one of a man, show evidence of burial rituals that suggest a belief in the afterlife. These early Australians lived beside the lake, eating Murray cod, golden perch, mussels, emu eggs, and a variety of marsupials, some of which were baked in earth ovens. They had stone scrapers, grinders and spear tips, and bone-barbed fish harpoons.

Today, some Aboriginal elders state that their people have always lived in Australia since the beginning of the human race, while other northern Aboriginals believe that the ancestral beings came from over the seas to the north. Some scholars believe that, during the last ice age when sea levels were lower, people from South-East Asia crossed a land bridge into Australia.

Wherever they came from, the Aboriginals have been here for at least 2000 generations. In that time they have lived in harmony with the land, something that seems to be extremely difficult for so-called civilised people, with a technology perfectly adapted to life in an often harsh and inhospitable country.

Long before the European invasion of their land, the Aboriginal people had been visited by Indonesians in search of trepang, pearl and tortoise shell. They bartered metal tools, food and clothing; and new techniques, ideas, words and concepts began to spread south. But on the morning of 20 April 1770, Captain James Cook and his crew on the *Endeavour* sighted land near the south-eastern tip of the mainland, changing the future of the Aboriginal people forever.

Earlier in the seventeenth century the Dutch had, at different times, landed at various points on the west coast of Australia, but finding no gold or spices, they lost interest. So, on 22 August 1770, there was nobody to argue when Cook took possession of the whole east coast in the name of England and called it New South Wales. Two hundred years later, in a symbolic protest, an Aboriginal landed in England and took possession of it for the Aboriginal people.

On the strength of vague reports about the week Cook's men spent in Botany Bay, Arthur Phillip was sent to Australia to found a penal settlement. He arrived ahead of the other convict ships on 18 January 1788, but finding Botany Bay unsuitable, he moved to the deep harbour of Port Jackson and began the daunting task of establishing a settlement. Only 250 of the 730 convicts were fit for work, and none of them had any knowledge of farming.

For two years the tiny group struggled with hunger, lack of provisions, equipment or clothing till the Second Fleet arrived. There were 300 women and 700 men amongst the convicts, and nearly 300 had died on the ship. Of the remainder, 500 were too sick to work, but there was food, and building supplies and equipment.

Slowly the settlement began to take shape, and by the end of 1792 a few stone buildings had been completed and the colony was close to self-sufficiency. Convicts continued to be transported till 1868, nearly 162 000 in all. Most landed in New South Wales or Van Diemen's Land in the 1820s and 1830s. Their average age was 26 years, 75 per cent were single, most were urban workers, 80 per cent were thieves, 16 per cent were women, 66 per cent were English, 33 per cent were Irish, and less than 20 per cent were Scots. The colonial experience brutalised both convicts and guards; punishment and liberality were random, but convicts *were* pardoned, and small land grants were used as a reward for emancipated convicts. Charles Darwin, who visited Sydney Town in 1836, said of the system that, by 'converting vagabonds, most useless in one hemisphere, into active citizens of another, and thus giving birth to a new and splendid country - a grand centre of civilization - it has succeeded to a degree perhaps unparalleled in history.' So much for adaptation!

From the 1820s, free settlers began to flock into the colony in search of land. Many who became squatters had reasonable capital, but for a fee of ten pounds per year plus a penny a head for stock, people with meagre funds were also able to take up land. Grasslands the size of France were taken up in an orderly but speedy manner, and by 1825, 148 800 kilograms of wool were exported to Britain. By 1840, wool exports had reached 3.5 million kilograms. Tragically, as settlement spread, the inevitable clashes between whites and Aboriginals resulted in increasing numbers of deaths. By 1876 the last full-blooded Tasmanian Aboriginal was dead, and mainland Aboriginals fared only slightly better.

Aboriginal rock paintings, Kakadu, Northern Territory

Aboriginal rock paintings, Kakadu, Northern Territory

Aboriginal rock paintings, Kakadu, Northern Territory

Port Arthur, penal settlement, Tasmania

Shot tower, Hobart, Tasmania

Spike Bridge, east coast of Tasmania

Early homestead, north-east Victoria

Early corrugated home, Broken Hill, New South Wales

Run-down homestead, Mornington Peninsula, Victoria

The People

Some say the Australian population has always been made up of migrants. But whether or not the first Australians - the Aboriginal people - migrated to the continent or sprang up here out of the earth, since 1788 the population has been made up of a collection of people of many different nationalities. At first, Aboriginals outnumbered Europeans by more than 300 to 1, but this soon changed as the native people succumbed to violence, disease, poison and despair, and successive waves of white invaders entered the country. By the first official census in 1828, the non-Aboriginal population had grown to more than 36 000 in New South Wales, and almost half of them were convicts.

The first Chinese came to Australia early, as labourers in 1828, but efforts to encourage more Asian workers were defeated by local opposition. This could have been the first stirrings of an ugly antipathy for Asians that resulted in bans on non-European labour, anti-Chinese riots on the goldfields, and the White Australia Policy.

In 1839, the first shipload of free immigrants arrived in Port Phillip on the *David Clark*; most of them were Scots. The next decade added French-Canadian prisoners, Welsh convicts, and refugees from Hungary and Germany fleeing political disorder. George Morphesis, one of the first Greeks to come to Australia, established a precedent by settling in Melbourne, now described as the biggest Greek city outside Athens!

Despite anti-Chinese feelings, the goldrush of the 1850s drew over 20 000 Chinese to the goldfields. By 1859, 20 per cent of all males were Chinese.

Enriching this polyglot mix still further, was an Afghan camel driver (the first of several hundred) who was brought to Australia for the Burke and Wills expedition into the desert. In the far north, Pacific island (or kanaka) labour was being indentured or kidnapped to work in Queensland. By federation in 1901 there were over 9000 islanders in that state, but all bar 1000 were later deported. Queensland actively encouraged Swedes and Norwegians to settle there with a free-passage scheme during the 1870s, and in the last quarter of the century, small numbers of Japanese worked on the Australian pearling luggers on the other side of the continent at Broome. It was hazardous work, and many of them never survived to return to Japan. Within the same twenty-five years, Russian, Spanish, Italian, Maltese and Lebanese settlers arrived.

Despite this variety, the 1901 census showed a population of 3.8 million non-Aboriginal people, of whom 96 per cent were born in Australia, New Zealand, or Britain. This particular ethnic mix was enshrined in that year in the notorious White Australia Policy, which excluded Chinese and other non-Caucasians, or for that matter anyone else the government chose to exclude, by simply administering a dictation test in a language in which they were bound to fail.

Some Italian migrants arrived in the 1920s, but until the Second World War brought floods of European refugees to Australia, most migrants continued to come from Britain. After the war, Maltese, Dutch, Italian, German, Austrian, Greek, American, Finnish, Swiss, Swedish, Norwegian, Danish, Baltic, Hungarian and Spanish people came either as assisted migrants or under special schemes.

These migrants did not always receive a ready welcome, even though, in theory, Australians sympathised with the plight of European refugees, opposed anti-Semitism, and appreciated that Australia's population had to grow, and grow rapidly. Migrants were all very well, so long as they lived in another neighbourhood, spoke faultless English, and did their utmost to become Australian in thought, word, deed, dress, and cuisine! Australians ate lots of plain overcooked meat and vegetables, and drank beer or tea: coffee was American, wine was European or sissy, anything with herbs or spices other than those used to stuff the Sunday chook was treated with suspicion. Spaghetti, let alone other forms of pasta, was considered dangerously exotic. Refugees found themselves derisively labelled as reffos, wogs, dagoes, balts, jugos, chows, boongs, chinks, yanks, fritzes or poms; and this habit of name-calling has persisted, so that each new wave of immigrants has had to suffer their own insulting labels.

Despite many Australians' impatience with all things foreign, their ignorance of other cultures, their inability to speak other languages or step far beyond the boundary of their own family traditions, the great experiment has worked. Even on the most superficial level - the food we eat - immigration has changed what it means to be Australian. Even the most xenophobic nationalist enjoys pizza, 'Chinese food', and spaghetti! The largest voluntary organised movement of people ever has succeeded not only in finding homes for countless thousands, but in changing Australia from the insular country it had been to a rich and lively nation.

But during these years the Aboriginal people continued to fare badly. The population dwindled from around 300 000 in 1788 to a mere 70 000 in 1947. Aboriginals were not even counted in the census till 1971, so all figures are estimates. By 1978, Aboriginals made up one per cent of the population, an increase at last.

The 1970s also witnessed the introduction of the first immigration policy not based on racial discrimination, thus ending the White Australia Policy in 1974. This change is slowly being reflected in the Australian population.

What has, to a greater or lesser extent, always been true of Australia, has now been formalised in the government policy of multiculturalism, which aims to provide equal opportunities for all racial groups, and to encourage the maintenance of different cultural heritages within Australia.

Face painting and costume for traditional Aboriginal dance, Northern Territory

Young Aborigines, South Australia

Aboriginal elder, Northern Territory

21

Asian Australian

European Australian

Aussie with well worn Akubra hat

22

Young surf-lifesavers, Sydney

Young Fijian Australian

Young Asian Australian

Outback mining, western Queensland

Industries

Viewed in isolation from the rest of the world, Australia is blessed: our farmers are amongst the most efficient in the world, and produce enough food to ensure self-sufficiency plus a surplus for export. There are vast mineral and energy resources, the political climate is stable, the Australian people are well-educated and capable - in fact all the ingredients for a healthy economy and flourishing industries are available. As Australia takes its place as a player in the strange game of world economics, it remains to be seen whether it has the skills necessary to thrive.

For most of its history, Australia has been considered a primary producer; indeed it seems to be almost a national failing to believe that the earth will endlessly provide, be it wheat, wool, beef, minerals, oil or natural gas. Australian sheep produce most of the world's best wool today, but only after years of struggle to establish breeds that were well adapted to poor, dry pastures, climatic extremes, pests and disease and could still produce fine fleeces. Elizabeth Macarthur is the mother of Australia's sheep industry. With her husband John (who spent many years away in England) she pioneered the industry with their merino flocks.

Like wool, wheat succeeded only after suitable strains and techniques were developed for the peculiar Australian conditions. And beef cattle had to be specially bred to survive the dry inland conditions where one cow per acre was all the land could support. To overcome the problems of distant beef markets, Victoria developed refrigeration, and in 1879 the first ship left for the lucrative London markets with a cargo of refrigerated meat.

In Queensland, sugarcane was first grown in 1847. Within 20 years, kanaka labour was being indentured to work in the plantations, a trade in humans which was later outlawed. The cane beetle that threatened crops was successfully wiped out by the introduction of giant cane toads which are now themselves a nuisance. In South Australia, New South Wales and Victoria, vineyards flourished, and Australian wines began to win international prizes, astonishing judges with their strength and 'big' flavours. When the deadly disease phyloxera wiped out the vines, new resistant rootstocks were planted, and today Australian wines are again receiving the recognition they deserve.

Cotton, rice, fruits, vegetables, plantation timber, fishing... Australia's primary industries are amongst the richest in the world. With the increasing respect for the land and its resources now emerging to counteract years of neglect and ignorance, Australia should continue to be the lucky country.

Industrially, Australia catered for little more than its own needs before the Second World War. In 1939, roughly half a million workers were employed in manufacturing, only 20 per cent more than at the end of the Depression. Five years after the end of the war, the figure had almost doubled. The manufacture of ships, munitions, aircraft, instruments, machinery and chemicals expanded during the war years. BHP, Australia's largest company, had begun operating its steelworks in 1915 at Newcastle, thirty years after boundary rider Charles Rasp established the company. After the war it grew rapidly, enjoying near monopoly trading conditions till at least the late 1950s, and diversifying into shipping, oil, natural gas, and gold.

No aluminium was produced in Australia till 1955, and till 1960, bauxite had to be imported. Then, huge deposits of bauxite were discovered on the Gove Peninsular, and by 1963, Australia was self-sufficient in aluminium.

Foreign capital poured into Australia for these new industries - at first British and American, and more recently Japanese. Exploration for oil and natural gas increased, more petroleum refineries were built, fertiliser plants, chemical and pharmaceutical factories were built and machine tools and electronic equipment production increased. Australia's car industry was also born after the war with the first Holden, built by a company who started as coach builders. The domestic appliance industry also flourished, encouraged by the consumer boom of the 1950s and the large influx of migrants.

Today Australia's manufacturing industries are having to face stiff competition from energetic new industrial powers overseas. There is increasing pressure to look beyond the reliable primary products that have supported the country in the past to new technologies and value-added industries. Tourism is a case in point. Growing at a rate of 30 per cent a year, supported overseas by Australian actors, film-makers and artists, and at home by an increasingly sophisticated service industry, tourism should be one of Australia's big earners in future.

Australia's airlines, which have developed into the world's best and safest passenger carriers, continue to do well; the local publishing industry has produced giants like Rupert Murdoch; breweries have grown large enough to challenge companies in what was once the 'motherland'; oil and gas production have made energy imports a thing of the past. As Australia approaches the twenty-first century it cannot afford to be complacent, but it can afford a little pride in what it has already achieved.

Iron-ore mining, Mt. Tom Price, Western Australia

Outback fuel delivery, Northern Territory

Modern building industries, Victoria

Underwater observatory, Green Island, Queensland

Australia's expanding tourist industry

Reef tours, Great Barrier Reef, Queensland

Peaceful tropical holiday, Heron Island, Queensland

Wheat farming, western Victoria

Vineyard, McLaren Vale, South Australia

Cider-apple growing, Tasmania

Swanston street, Melbourne, Victoria

The Cities

Sydney is the oldest and largest of Australia's cities, founded in 1788 by a collection of convicts and soldiers who had come to establish a penal colony. Sydney Harbour is one of the loveliest in the world, and the city never quite loses its air of holiday fun and frivolity, basking in the sunshine beside the glittering blue of the sea. Sydneysiders can take a ferry to work, and on weekends the water is dotted with the colourful sails and spinnakers of yachts. The famous landmarks of the Opera House and Sydney Harbour Bridge are reflected day and night in the Harbour waters, just opposite the gaudy colours of the funfare Luna Park.

The city centre is brash and modern, and nearby is bawdy brassy Kings Cross with its strippers and bars. But there are still many pockets of early Sydney with graceful Georgian stone houses, winding streets, and surprising little patches of bush or park tucked away at the water's edge. Sydney is a tourist's paradise, where every taste is catered for and leisure is almost a profession.

Unlike Sydney, Melbourne is one of the few major Australian cities to be founded as a free settlement rather than a penal centre. It was settled in 1835, when John Batman announced with prescience if not confidence, 'This will be the place for a village.' It was only twenty years before the goldrush transformed it from a small town to an established city of wide streets, impressive Victorian buildings, and graceful parks and gardens.

Melbourne was a planned city, like Adelaide, laid out on a grid pattern just north of the Yarra River. At federation, Melbourne became the capital city, having already established itself as the centre for banking, commerce, industry and defense. Melburnians would argue that Melbourne is still the intellectual and cultural capital at least, and some particularly partisan inhabitants make even stronger claims.

Canberra, the national capital, was formally launched in 1927 with the opening of the new national parliament. It had been planned for years, and an international competition was held to choose the best design. Walter Burley Griffin won with a design for a garden city with sweeping harmonious curves and circles rather than rectangular grids, where gardens and parks are at least as important as buildings.

With the completion of the fine National Gallery, High Court Building, and (new new) Parliament House, all precisely sited on the opposite side of Lake Burley Griffin from the War Memorial, Griffin's vision is being vindicated.

Queensland's capital, Brisbane, lies on the edge of the tropics beside the largest commercial river in Australia. Basking in an average of nearly eight hours of sunshine a day, Brisbane's inhabitants have adopted a casual relaxed style, with fifty square kilometres set aside for parks, gardens, recreation and forest reserves. This way of life could be traditional, because Brisbane took its time about developing. Founded in 1824, the population had grown to a mere five thousand by 1859 when Queensland was declared a separate state. Today the skyline is like any modern city's, but the gardens still abound with tropical flowers and fruits, and there is always time for a quiet talk over a cool beer on a shady verandah.

Amongst its early colonial counterparts, Adelaide is the only thoroughly planned city. Its fine streets are balanced by beautiful gardens and parks, and boast some of the most delightful colonial stone buildings in the country. Although the city has a reputation for being staid, it is the head of a surprisingly progressive state, quietly winning for itself the role of cultural leader with its biennial Arts Festival.

Perth, the only city on the west coast, was founded in 1829, and is separated from the rest of Australia by vast stretches of desert and salt-lake country. It is Australia's sunniest capital, situated on the lovely Swan River, named early after the abundant black swans that were sighted by Willem de Vlamingh in 1697.

The immense mineral wealth of the state is reflected in the city's growing affluence, but this modern 'boom town' has managed to preserve much of its past. Less surprisingly, this city by the water has become a yachting mecca since the Americas Cup challenge was held here.

Hobart, second oldest city in Australia, is the capital of the island state of Tasmania. It was established in 1804, and perhaps because of this, or because it has remained relatively small, it has retained a distinctly English air. Set in magnificent scenery on the banks of the blue Derwent River beneath the impressive bulk of Mount Wellington, the city is a treasure trove of historic buildings.

At the other end of the continent is Darwin, capital of the Northern Territory. Devastated in a cyclone at Christmas in 1974, the city has been almost completely rebuilt. Situated on the doorstep of Asia, with an Aboriginal population that seems to have suffered slightly less from the European invasion (if only because it was delayed by isolation), Darwin's population is the most diverse.

A tropical climate enforces a relaxed way of life, and much of the architecture pays homage to the heat. The new city's affluence and energy is perhaps symbolised by the new casino, roughly two thousand kilometres north-west of its Tasmanian counterpart.

The Harbour Bridge and Opera House at night

Hydrofoil, Sydney Harbour

Sydney, New South Wales

Sydney Tower at night

Sunset over the Westgate Bridge

Melbourne, Victoria

Evening along St. Kilda Road

Melbourne skyline over the Yarra River

Hobart from Mt. Wellington

Market Day, Salamanca Place

Hobart, Tasmania

Hobart and the Tasman Bridge

Colonel Light and city skyline

Adelaide, South Australia

Rundle Street Mall, Adelaide

Victoria Square fountain

Perth sky-line at dusk from Kings Park

Multicultural Freemantle

Perth, Western Australia

Perth sky-line at night

Todd River race, Alice Springs

Darwin and Alice Springs, Northern Territory

The city of Darwin

Alice Springs township

Twilight, Surfers Paradise, Gold Coast

Story Bridge, Brisbane

Brisbane and the Gold Coast, Queensland

Town Hall, Brisbane

The new Parliament House, Australian Capital Territory

Canberra, Australian Capital Territory

Capital Hill from Mt. Ainslie, Australian Capital Territory

Canberra across Lake Burley-Griffin, Australian Capital Territory

50

Morning mist, South Gippsland, Victoria

Rural Life

Agriculture got off to a slow start in Australia after European settlement, partly because of the site chosen by the First Fleet, partly because of the lack of human or animal muscle-power, and partly because of ignorance. At first it was far more profitable to reap the bounty of the forests and seas, and to set up pastoral enterprises rather than grow the food crops so desperately needed by the early settlers.

Pastoralists put pressure on the available grazing land, and soon explorers were heading into the wilderness in search of new grasslands on which Australia's first great industries - wool and meat - were to be based. Settlement slowly spread as explorers and squatters opened up country in Queensland, what would be Victoria, South Australia, and Western Australia. Tasmania had been settled early as a penal colony.

Everywhere a hopelessly uneven war was waged against the Aboriginals who attempted to defend their land against the white invaders, but disease, guns, poison and despair took their toll. Squatting families too suffered in this undeclared war, but to a much lesser extent. At first they made do with rough bark or slab shelters while they set about clearing, and often over-clearing the land of its tree cover. Isolation made all the hazards of life so much greater, both for the squatting families and for their convict or ticket-of-leave labourers.

By 1845, the shaky future of wool farming was looking a little brighter, but within about a decade, the discovery of gold put the thought of sheep out of most people's minds and changed the face of Australia forever. The population increased dramatically, and for farmers and traders who kept their heads and supplied the diggers rather than rushing off to the goldfields themselves, there were fortunes to be made.

Slowly the dry inland was taken up too, with cattle roaming free of fences over holdings measured in tens of kilometres rather than acres. Because of the scarcity of water, stock were relatively easy to locate and control, and small teams of drovers were able to travel with cattle across vast distances. The hardy independent drover entered our folklore, along with the little battlers who clung for a time to land just beyond the zone of reasonable regular rainfall, failed, left in despair to be replaced perhaps by another family of hopeful farmers. Bush life and bush characters became synonymous with Australians, despite the fact that most Australians lived in the cities.

After the goldrush, many of the diggers turned to farming, and 'selectors' - small farmers who selected land, sometimes in the best country or around waterholes - became the bane of the established squatters. The battle raged between wealthy squatters and poorer selectors, most of whom had to rely on family labour because they could not afford to hire help. Transport was primitive, and life was hard at first.

From 1860 to 1890 huge areas of land were opened up for settlement, labour supply improved, and in the older settled areas transport became more reliable. By 1861 there were twenty million sheep in Australia. By 1870, wool was the biggest export earner, and shearers began to challenge drovers in the popular imagination. Early experiments with wheat were not so successful however, until people realised that the Old World strains were not suitable for Australian conditions and that Australia's ancient soils were lacking in phosphates. Much later, the introduction of super-phosphate, new strains of wheat, and later the tractor and sophisticated seeding and harvesting machines began to produce results. Today Australia is amongst the top wheat producers in the world.

The last decade of the nineteenth century was disastrous for farmers in Australia. Economic depression hit, rabbits destroyed pastures in the outback, and a severe drought reduced sheep numbers dramatically. In the century that was to follow, two world wars and another severe depression in the 1930s changed country life forever. Aircraft and heavy machinery were introduced, forests razed, transport improved, drovers replaced by enormous road trains. Smaller farms were amalgamated to make feasible the heavy investment in plant, and large-scale farming became common.

Wool, wheat, and beef are still good export earners for Australia, but in recent years more imaginative schemes have broadened the base of Australia's agriculture. Today, with much of Australia's fertile soil under threat from over-stocking and greedy intensive farming methods in the past, some farmers are slowly learning to treat the land with respect. The destruction of forests is now hotly debated, and the wholesale use of chemicals in agriculture is becoming unpopular. The isolation of bush life has been overcome in part by technology, but country people still value the qualities that make them different from their city cousins.

Lush pasture, South Gippsland, Victoria

Sheep droving, New South Wales

Cattle mustering, north east Victoria

Country mailboxes, north east Victoria

Sheep grazing, central New South Wales

Cattle country, South Australia

Cattle grazing, southern New South Wales

Morning mists, Myrtleford, north-eastern Victoria

Water pump and outbuildings, southern Queensland

Fun-run

Sporting Traditions

European settlement in Australia is barely two hundred years old, but in that short time the relatively tiny population has produced an inordinate number of sporting stars. In proportion to population, Australia has more victories in international competitions than all other countries, including Russia and America. In the first Olympics in 1896, Australian E. H. Flack won the 800m and the 1500m. Only in the 1904 Olympics did Australia fail to win a place - after that, the list of prizes grew steadily longer. Some believe the climate, the facilities, and even the traditional high-protein diet of Australians account for their success in sport. In almost every field there have been Australian champions:

swimming - Tracy Wickham, Michelle Ford, Shane Gould, Dawn Fraser, John Konrads

running - Robert DeCastella, Herb Elliot, Ron Clarke, John Landy

cricket - Dennis Lillee, Alan Border, Don Bradman, Charlie McCartney, Richie Benaud

golf - Greg Norman, Peter Thomson, Kel Nagle, Bruce Devlin

tennis - Pat Cash, Margaret Court, Evonne Goolagong Cawley, Rod Laver, Ken Rosewall

boxing - Dave Sands, Les Darcy, Lionel Rose, Jimmy Carruthers, Johnny Famechon, Jeff Fenech

cycling - Hubert Opperman, Phillip Anderson

motor racing - Jack Brabham, Alan Jones

surfing - Ian Cairns, Mark Andrews, Mark Richards

weight-lifting - Dean Lukin.

Australia has also had champions in most of the track-and-field athletic events, polo, yachting (including the 1983 Americas Cup), billiards, snooker, rugby and hockey.

Perhaps it is simply love of sport that produces so many stars. For many Australians, sport is almost a religion, be they spectators or players, and Australians play a greater variety of sports than any other nation in the world. Most of these sports have been imported, but some, such as Australian Rules football, boomerang throwing, sheep shearing, skiing, speedway racing and 2-up are local inventions.

Speedway or dirt track racing originated in Maitland in 1925, then spread to Britain. Skiing had an even earlier start, and the sport has a longer history in Australia than in Switzerland, where it began late in the mid 1890s. In 1862 skiing was already an established sport at Kiandra, and the ski club there is one of the oldest in the world. Another first for Australia was the invention of the Australian Crawl by Richard Cavill, one of a family of six excellent swimmers and son of Fred Cavill who swam the English Channel in 1877. In his day, Dick Cavill was virtually unbeatable, and was the first man to ever swim 100 yards in less than a minute.

Unbeatable in another field was Walter Lindrum, who, like Cavill, came from a family who excelled at their sport - in this case billiards. Lindrum was the unbeaten world champion billiards player for 26 years, and when he retired in 1950, he held 57 world records.

A four-legged Australian (born in New Zealand) became the country's darling in the bleak years of the Depression - Phar Lap, the racehorse who won the Melbourne Cup in 1930, plus 36 other races out of 52 starts. After his death in America from accidental poisoning, his heart, hide and skeleton were preserved and are now displayed in Canberra, Melbourne and New Zealand respectively. Incidentally, the Melbourne Cup is Australia's greatest horse race, and Melburnians enjoy a public holiday because of it - declared by act of parliament!

A less uplifting event during the Depression was the English cricket team's introduction of bodyline bowling in an attempt to stop the previously unstoppable champion Don Bradman. English bowlers bowled short so that the ball would bounce up at the batsman's head, shoulders and chest, forcing him to defend himself. As the list of injured Australian batsmen grew, diplomatic relations became strained, and after the series a law was passed banning the practice. The history of Anglo-Australian cricket had begun in 1861 when the British sent a team to Australia. All work stopped, and parliament was adjourned. An Australian team returned to England, made up entirely of full-blooded Aboriginals.

But football is perhaps *the* Australian game, and despite the publicity surrounding the native Australian Rules football, three imported forms of football are also popular - Rugby League, Rugby Union and Soccer. In the states where Australian Rules football is played, and especially in Victoria, the game is more like a cult than a sport. In what other country, at what other game would crowds of over 100 000 people turn out for a grand final?

Surf boat, New South Wales

Pre-race time, Sydney to Hobart yacht race

Big surf, Margaret River, Western Australia

Spring racing carnival, Melbourne, Victoria

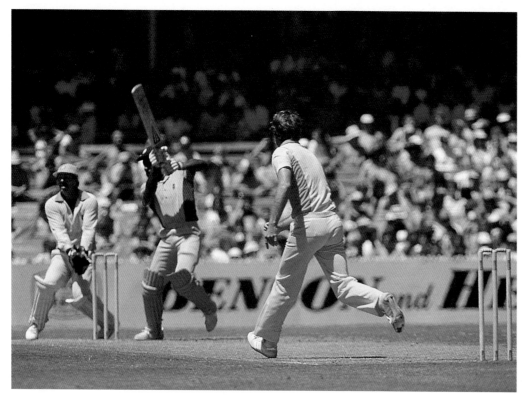

World Cup cricket, M.C.G. Melbourne, Victoria

Australian Rules Football, Melbourne, Victoria

65

Mail run to outback station, Queensland

The Outback

Dryness and heat characterise the Outback, a region in the heart of Australia that stretches 2000 kilometres from north to south and 2500 kilometres from east to west. The Great Sandy Desert, Gibson Desert, Great Victorian Desert and Nullarbor Plain are to the west, and to the east is the Simpson Desert which joins Sturt's Stony Desert. North-west of Alice Springs is the Tanami Desert.

Unlike the Sahara, Australia's deserts are usually not endless expanses of sand, but sparsely vegetated dunes and clay or salt pans. In other areas patchy grasslands are replaced with savannah, and dry creek beds are often marked by stunted eucalypts and acacias. Mulga scrublands give way to gibber-stone plains, and the flat expanses are punctuated by rough rocky ranges - the Northern Flinders, Petermann, Musgrave and MacDonnells - and the peculiar domes of the Olgas (Katajuta) and Ayers Rock (Uluru). The Rock, which rises dramatically from a seemingly endless plain to a height of 348 metres, consists of coarse sandstone, deposited underwater as ancient mountain ranges eroded 600 million years ago. Later, the earth tilted the sandstone almost vertically, and the Rock itself began to erode in turn. About 110 million years ago it would have been an island, lapped at its base by waves that created the caves dotted around its massive bulk. No photograph or film can ever prepare a visitor for their first sight of that red mammoth!

Years of drought can bake and scorch the red earth of the Outback till it is hard to believe that any living thing could survive. Gibber plains glitter under the stark blue sky, and in the mulga scrub the dead bones of stunted bushes bleach and whiten. Dust devils dance over the plains lifting the dry sand into airy columns, and the silence is only broken by the occasional forlorn cawing of a crow.

But when the rain does come, and eventually it does, sometimes in abundance, the barren land is transformed into a garden. In the pools and waterholes, eggs that have survived years of drought hatch,and species of primitive shrimp appear, the first link in a food chain of unexpected plenty. On the bare sand beneath stunted trees and shrubs, a veil of green appears. Soon masses of flowers carpet the earth with pink, white, yellow, red and cream, many of them the papery everlastings that dry but do not wilt when picked.

Birds are quick to take advantage of these improved conditions, and will often migrate to areas of good rains in order to breed where an abundance of insect life ensures the survival of their chicks. Bird populations increase rapidly, first by migration, then by breeding. Insects, reptiles and desert mammals all make the most of these short patches of favourable conditions to ensure at least another generation will survive.

Over the last few hundred million years, the ridges of the desert's backbone have been worn away by wind, ice and water from a towering chain of mountains to a series of ranges with only a few peaks reaching over 1000 metres. These ranges have witnessed dramatic swings in climate and vegetation, from the damp rich rainforests that once covered the outback to the dessicating cooling winds of the ice ages that dried up the lakes and killed the forests. Only in Palm Valley near Alice Springs can remnants of this ancient vegetation be seen. In the permanent dampness along the creek, protected from the worst of the desert winds, grow unique palms.

Elsewhere it is very difficult for anything to grow or survive, and for every vast cattle station that has managed to scratch a living out of the barren soil, others have been abandoned. Mining companies have pushed roads and tracks across the desert and burrowed into the ranges, but despite this, much of the Outback is still wilderness.

Olgas, Northern Territory

Sunset, Olgas, Northern Territory

Entry to the Valley of the Winds, Olgas, Northern Territory

Ross River homestead, Northern Territory

Wave Rock, Hyden, Western Australia

King's Canyon, Northern Territory

71

Katherine Gorge, lower reaches, Northern Territory

Jedda Rock, Katherine Gorge, Northern Territory

Katherine Gorge, Northern Territory

Uluru (Ayers Rock), Northern Territory

Climbing face, Uluru (Ayers Rock), Northern Territory

Sunrise, aerial view, Uluru (Ayers Rock), Northern Territory

Iron ore country, Western Australia

The Macdonnell Ranges, Northern Territory

Wittenoom Gorge, The Pilbara, north-west Western Australia

Afternoon shadows, Victorian coastline

Islands and Coastline

Ringed by seven seas, Australia's coastline has been shaped by wind tide and weather. In places, sandy beaches flanked by dunes and combed by breakers extend for fifty or one hundred kilometres. The north-west of Western Australia, South Australia's Coorong, and the Gippsland coasts of Victoria are renowned for unbroken stretches of beach. In less dramatic lengths, these white or golden sandy beaches occur round most of the continent. Punctuating these sandy stretches are huge cliffs, battered by storms rolling undisturbed across the Southern Ocean from the Antarctic. The cliffs of the Great Australian Bight stretching to the horizon are typical of this landform. Further east, the cliffs, arches, stacks and monoliths of the Twelve Apostles on the Victorian coast near Port Campbell have also felt the bite of the Southern Ocean.

Tasmania is again the exception to most of the rules that apply to the mainland's coast. It has perhaps the most dramatic coastal scenery, formed in the south-east by towering serrated cliffs of columnar dolerite, a hard volcanic stone that resists weathering, and in the south-west by thick rainforest tumbling down to the jagged rock walls and headlands that break the force of ocean swells. Tasmania, itself an island state, has its own share of islands, all of them drowned mountaintops that share the rugged grandeur of the rest of the coast.

Back over Bass Strait, King and Flinders Islands, to Victoria, and the Great Ocean Road which continues east along the Otway Ranges through coastal hills beside inlets, sandy beaches or rocky cliffs. Similar variety can be seen on the Cook Highway between Cairns and Port Douglas, and in between along the south coast of New South Wales are many calm estuaries and inlets popular with anglers and holidaymakers.

Further north is the world's largest and most unusual sand island - Fraser Island. The sand of this island not only supports rainforest, but also freshwater lakes. Originating in the mountains of New South Wales to the south, the sands have gradually been carried north by the waves and deposited along sandy beaches and sand islands. Beyond Fraser Island, the Great Barrier Reef protects the coast and reduces the amount of sand shifted. Many of these sandy beaches, dunes and islands are protected as National Parks, although at one stage, Fraser Island itself was threatened by sand mining.

Further north again, the Great Barrier Reef - 2000 kilometres of coral - protects the coast from Pacific swells. A vast and complex maze of reefs, islands and passages, this natural wonder supports a delicately balanced ecology where beautiful fish, crabs, corals, sea stars and urchins, sponges, worms and weeds of extraordinary colour and variety flourish. In this region, most of Australia's islands occur, many of them as close to an earthly paradise as it is possible to imagine. The largest are mountains covered in rich vegetation, drowned when the last ice age ended. There are also several hundred cays formed of sand and coral rubble, home to a variety of grasses, plants and trees, depending on their size. Free from mainland predators, the islands also support many varieties of birds in large numbers.

In the far north of Australia, low coastal plains lined with tangled mangroves slip gradually into a warm sea as the tide creeps imperceptibly up and down during the day. The water is often muddied by the thick silty waters of the rivers after each Wet. An inhospitable coast with biting poisonous insects, fish and crocodiles, it rings some of Australia's most spectacular tropical country.

Further west is the rugged coast of the north-west Kimberley region, dotted with islands and almost inaccessible from either land or sea, but magnificent from the air.

Four-mile beach, Port Douglas, Queensland

Hardy's Reef, Great Barrier Reef, Queensland

Low Island, Great Barrier Reef, Queensland

81

Heron Island, Queensland

Lizard Island, far north Queensland

Beach near Cairns, Queensland

Flying over Whitsunday Passage, Queensland

Cedar Bay, Cooktown, Queensland

Hinchinbrook Island, Whitsundays, Queensland

Whitsunday sunset from South Molle Island, Queensland

Late afternoon, Whitsunday Passage, Queensland

Whitsunday Islands from Mackay, Queensland

Freycinet Peninsula, east coast of Tasmania

Philip Island coastline, Victoria

Basalt cliffs, Tasman Island

Grampians, north-west Victoria

The Mountains

Australia is an ancient land - one needs only to look at it to know that. Its volcanoes are worn to hills or eroded to volcanic plugs, its great folds and buckles have been scraped away by aeons of wind and water. Sitting in the middle of a huge rock plate, it has slowly drifted north like a frog on a lily pad, protected from the upheavals that have created the world's mountains as one massive plate grinds against another.

The highest peaks in the Snowy Mountains barely exceed 2000 metres, and less than five per cent of land is above 600 metres. These 'alps' are the highest point in a chain of mountains formed two or three million years ago - the Great Dividing Range - which run for 5000 kilometres from Cape York in the north down the east coast of Australia to Victoria. Their last outstation is the scenic Grampians, a floral laboratory where it is possible to see nature experimenting with apparently endless varieties of colour, shape, and size.

Along the length of the Great Divide are many different habitats - tropical, rain and cloud forests, temperate forests, scrub, farming land, sub-alpine and alpine - supporting a wealth of flora and fauna. To the east, moisture-laden clouds deposit rain on the slopes as the mountains force air currents up from the sea, but once over the Divide, the dryness that will characterise the country of the inland begins in the rainshadow of the ranges. It took the first white settlers 24 years to find a way across the bewildering rugged peaks and gorges that separated them from the inland. Some explorers barely survived, others were less fortunate.

Older mountain ranges, all formed originally by folding or faulting, include the Flinders Ranges in South Australia, the MacDonnell Ranges further north in the Northern Territory, and in the west the Kimberleys and Hamersley Ranges. Not a true mountain range, the escarpment of Arnhem Land in the Northern Territory is none the less one of the spectacles of Kakadu National Park - a vast art gallery where Aboriginal people have come to paint on the rocks for perhaps 40 000 years. In some cases, the paintings have outlasted their subjects - the thylacine, for example, is not only extinct on the mainland now, but since white settlement it has also disappeared from its last stronghold in Tasmania.

The Flinders Ranges contain some spectacularly beautiful scenery - saw-toothed sandstone ridges of warm red, blending to blues and purples in the distance.

Further north across gibber plains and desert is the world's largest rock - Uluru, or Ayers Rock as it is known to the whites. Nearby are the Olgas or Katajuta. Both are leftovers of a sandstone mass that underlies the surrounding plains. As Ayers Rock was thrust upwards, the mass tilted sideways so that the sedimentary layers run almost vertically up from the plain, resulting in more or less uniform weathering. The Olgas however are formed of a rough conglomerate which has been carved into huge balls and domes by the action of water and wind. Both share the spectacular glowing colours of the inland.

Another oddity in the Western Kimberleys in Western Australia is an ancient coral barrier reef, the grey limestone of which now forms the Napier Range. Cut by the Lennard River, the Windjana Gorge bisects the range and gives the national park its name. But the most bizarre formation occurred when an enormous missile from outer space scored a bullseye in the centre of Australia. At Gosse's Bluff, the crater formed by this monstrous impact has long since eroded, but the rock that spewed up at the point of impact from almost three kilometres underground survives and forms the bluff. It is 200 metres high and 5 kilometres wide - a massive bullet wound on the earth's hide.

Equally dramatic, if more conventional in origin are the mountain wilderness areas in Tasmania, where volcanoes, uplifts and extensive glaciation have formed magnificent peaks and sharp jagged ridges. For Australians, this country is closer to real mountain country - afterall, these mountains finish in sharp points rather than blunt eroded curves! In Tasmania too are extensive stretches of beautiful alpine pasture rivaling that of the Australian Alps on the mainland with the complexity and subtlety of it vegetation.

Binnaburra, southern Queensland

Towards Mt. William, western Victoria

Cathedral Mountain mists, central Victoria

92

Mt. Roland, northern Tasmania

Mt. Lyell, Queenstown, south-west Tasmania

Mt. Roland, northern Tasmania

Thredbo, southern New South Wales

Bogong High Plains, from the Ovens River

Giant snowdrift, southern New South Wales

96

Mt. Nelson, south-west Tasmania

Rainforests

Australia had 15 per cent tree cover before European settlement; now it has 3 per cent. Of the once extensive rainforests, less than 1 per cent remains of the virgin rainforest that once covered much of Cape York; there is a narrow strip that runs from Cardwell to Cooktown, in northern Queensland and after that only isolated patches. That rainforest continues to be cleared in Queensland is a crime not only against humanity, but against the earth, for once it has gone it cannot regenerate, and the rainforest creatures cannot survive outside the intricate complex ecology of the rainforest. Unlike other forms of Australian bush and forest, rainforest does not regenerate after fires. A few hectares of tropical rainforest contains as many species of flora and fauna as all of Europe, many of them potentially useful to humans. But the forests are being destroyed before the species can even be identified, let alone fully understood.

There are three types of rainforest: tropical, subtropical and temperate. Only a narrow strip along the coast between Cooktown and Ingham in north Queensland still supports the lushest tropical rainforest. Other types are scattered along the north and east coasts from the Kimberleys and south to Tasmania. There are three major zones stretching from the higher altitudes in the warmer north to sea level in the colder south.

Rainforests are made up of many different species of plants dominated by towering trees that form a dense closed canopy. Unlike the more common eucalypts, rainforest plants are usually broad-leafed. Shrubs form a second layer, and lianes and epiphytes usually grow on and hang from the trees. The floor is covered in mosses and leaf litter.

Tropical rainforest is characterised by a dense almost unbroken canopy of multi-layered broad-leafed evergreen trees and vines. Below the canopy the air is humid, and only a little light filters through. Trees have prop or stilt roots or high buttresses, usually for stability. The leaves, often very large, are thin and smooth, and the flowers and fruit often grow not amongst the foliage, but lower down on the trunks and main branches (a phenomenon called 'cauliflory'). The vines and lianes, with their foliage high in the canopy, hang from branches and trail their stems to the forest floor. Epiphytic ferns and orchids grow on branches and trunks with no contact with the soil. Elkhorns and staghorns are common epiphytes, and the strangler tree starts life as an epiphyte high in the branches of a host tree. It sends down fine threadlike roots which gradually thicken and blend until it is capable of supporting itself. By this time it no longer needs the host tree, which has, by now, been killed or strangled.

Subtropical rainforests look similar to tropical rainforests but contain fewer species. Leaves are smaller, there are fewer buttressed trees, very few stilt roots and no cauliflory. Strangler trees still exist. These forests are more common further south or at higher altitudes in the north, and range (in patches) from Mossman on the top of the Coast Range in north Queensland down the eastern seabord to the south coast of New South Wales at ever decreasing altitudes.

Temperate rainforest begins in south Queensland in patches on the McPherson Range and continues both down the mountains to the coast and south along the coast through New South Wales, Victoria and Tasmania. The dominant species is the southern beech, with little variety in the understory apart from treeferns, or in Tasmania, horizontal scrub. The towering mountain ash, one of the tallest trees in the world, also grows in temperate rainforests. In Tasmania, the myrtle or Antarctic beech can top 50 metres, 20 metres taller than the sassafras which is noted for its fragrant bark and beautiful wood. On the forest floor, spongy sphagnum moss flourishes, soaking up 20 times its own weight in water.

Evergreen rainforests do not lose their leaves, but forests in dryer areas can shed their leaves during the dry season; in Tasmania, the forests turn to gold as the beech leaves colour up.

Most creatures and birds of the rainforest do not exist outside that rapidly shrinking environment. The Daintree is one of the largest continuous areas of rainforest remaining in Australia, but it is still threatened by greedy logging companies and apathetic politicians. In places the forested ranges reach down to the sea, a rare occurence in Australia where the coast is usually fringed by woodlands, heaths, swamps or mangroves.

Extraordinarily rich and complex biologically, over 1000 species of trees exist in the Daintree, including a unique primitive tree, *Idiospermium australiense*, which has created a new plant family and formed a link with the origins of flowering plants.

Mt. Field National Park, southern Tasmania

Lyell Highway, southern Tasmania

Mt. Nelson, south-west Tasmania

101

Fern gully, Dandenong Ranges, Victoria

Tree-fern, Dandenong Ranges, Victoria

Otway Ranges, south-west Victoria

Dense tropical rainforest, Daintree, northern Queensland

Mt. Tambourine, southern Queensland

Fraser Island, Queensland

Blue-tongue lizard

Wildflowers, Western Australia

Wildlife and Wildflowers

Australia's wildlife and wildflowers are not only more diverse than most other countries', many of the species are unique. Surprisingly, Australia has only four of the seventeen orders of mammals worldwide - marsupials, monotremes, rodents and bats - but all three of the orders of marine mammals - cetaceans (whales), seals and dugongs. But what it lacks in numbers of orders, it makes up for in diversity and rarity. For example, monotremes and two thirds of the world's marsupials occur only in Australia and New Guinea. The monotremes are egg-laying mammals that suckle their young - a combination that seems to take something from the reptiles and birds, and the rest from warm-blooded creatures. The echidna or spiny anteater is a fairly regular looking monotreme, but the platypus is bizarre: it is semi-aquatic, furred, with webbed feet and a bill like a duck. It lays eggs like a duck too, but no duck ever fed its ducklings on milk!

The marsupials of the world are born while still tiny, naked and underdeveloped. Somehow they make their way to their mother's pouch, attach themselves to a teat, and spend the rest of their developmental time growing in the pouch. The four natural groups include: the South American opossums; carnivorous Australian marsupials; omnivorous bandicoots and bilbies; and herbivorous possums and kangaroos. Two Australian oddities, the marsupial mole and the honey-possum, have to be placed in their own groups.

The carnivorous marsupials include the ferocious quolls; and the Tasmanian devil, whose jaws are strong enough to crack large kangaroo bones; the tiny but vicious mouse-like antechinuses; phascogales; dibblers; the apparently extinct Tasmanian tiger; termite-eating numbats; and the unique insectivorous marsupial mole.

Of the omnivorous bandicoots and bilbies, several species are either extinct or rare. Sometimes this has been due to disease or other natural causes, but all too often it has been because of feral animals introduced since white settlement or the systematic destruction of habitats.

One of the best-loved Australian herbivorous marsupials is the koala. This bear-like creature is the only arboreal animal that lacks a tail, a feature it shares with its close relative the terrestrial wombat. Koalas live exclusively on eucalyptus leaves, a diet unpalatable or even toxic to most mammals. During the day they doze in the fork of a tree, but just after sunset they begin to feed actively. Although the koala is harmless, the dreadful roars and groans of the males are amongst the most frightening noises in the bush at night.

Wombats are mostly nocturnal, especially during summer when they spend the hottest part of the day in a shady burrow. The common wombat is a forest dweller, and the hairy-nosed wombat a plains dweller. Although these loveable creatures have a reputation for being muddle-headed, they have large well-developed brains.

Australia's possums form another large family of fruit or leaf-eating marsupials ranging from the large brush-tails and cuscus, to the tiny pygmy possums. Gliders are equipped with a cloak-like membrane between fingers and feet on either side of the body which allows them to glide from tree to tree.

The kangaroo, Australia's mascot, belongs to a very large family of herbivores, all pouched, including the potoroos, wallabies, climbing tree kangaroos and pademelons. The young kangaroos or joeys live in their mothers' pouches until they are quite large, often leaning out to snatch a bite of grass when they are ready for 'solids'.

Apart from mammals, Australia is well-endowed with reptiles. There are over a hundred species of snakes, many of them extremely venomous. Fortunately some, like the beautiful python, are not. Lizards come in all shapes and sizes from huge goannas to tiny metallic skinks. The blue-tongue is a popular pet amongst country children, but the well-known frill-necked lizard is not so sociable. When approached or alarmed, it displays its umbrella-like neck ruff, thereby increasing its apparent size and frightening off potential threats. Frogs, turtles and tortoises are also well represented, and in the far north, harmless freshwater crocodiles inhabit the rivers and billabongs of the Top End. Their dangerous salt-water relatives are also numerous, but the salinity of a swimming pool is no guarantee of safety, for when the rivers flood in the Wet, the 'salties' can swim far inland.

Some of Australia's birds appear as freakish to Europeans as our animals. The swans are black instead of white, the shy dancing lyrebird can mimic cats, birds, or the crack of an axe, and the kookaburra laughs with a loud mocking cackle. The flightless emu makes up for it by running at speeds up to 48 kilometres per hour. She lays her eggs then leaves them in the care of her mate, who cares for them devotedly, rarely eating till they are hatched. He then broods the chicks at night and continues to care for them for up to 18 months. However the budgerigar, native to most of Australia except the coastal fringes, needs no introduction.

Many flowers are as unusual as Australia's wildlife. The aptly named kangaroo paws, spider orchids, flying duck or mosquito orchids mimic their namesakes; the sundews capture insects in sticky dewdrops; and the unique and lovely trigger flowers ensure fertilisation by capturing unsuspecting insects with a 'spring-loaded' pistil.

Fire is a commonplace in Australia, and many plants have adapted to it. Some will only germinate after a fire, while others, like the grass tree, flower more abundantly after fire.

Koala

Echidna

Kangaroo and joey

Dingo

Platypus

Wombat

111

Black swan and its young

Sulphur crested cockatoo

Emu and chicks

Bottlebrush

Kangaroo Paw

Wattle

115

Marshland, Port Fairy, western Victoria

Rivers and Lakes

Australia, known as the driest continent, has less rain than any other continent except Antarctica. Compared to similar landmasses, it has less than a quarter of the average run-off (water draining into the sea), and only the Murray-Darling river system ranks as a major river. This is due to its vast catchment area, which includes almost all of New South Wales and Victoria west and north of the Divide, and the southern third of Queensland west of the Divide, rather than the size of the river itself, which finally runs into the sea south of Adelaide.

Characteristically Australian rivers vary in flow, some disappearing altogether in the hot dry months of the year. Half of the continent has an annual rainfall of less than 250mm or 10 inches, and a third is so dry it's almost uninhabitable. A huge wedge of Australia bounded to the south by the Eyre Highway, to the west and north by the Great Northern Highway, and to the east by the Stuart Highway, has virtually no rivers, and the lakes are salt pans unless there is an exceptional amount of rain.

Almost 90 per cent of the rain that falls in Australia never reaches the sea - in the Centre there is little to prevent evaporation, and the sandy soils are greedy for moisture. The best of these inland rivers peter out into strings of water-holes in sandy beds, although sometimes water continues to flow beneath the surface.

But to the east of the continent is the Great Divide - a chain of mountain ranges that runs the entire length of the eastern coast. On its well-watered eastern slopes many fast permanent rivers flow to the sea. Some of them, especially the wild rivers of Tasmania, are ideal for white water canoing or rafting. Others are calmer and more peaceful, and attract visitors who enjoy fishing, swimming, bushwalking, boating or simply gazing at beautiful scenery.

On the drier western slopes of the Divide there are only a few large river systems like the Murray-Darling.

In the tropical northern Wet season, many great rivers such as the Herbert and Burdekin are fed from the torrential rains that fall on the mountains of the Divide and their rainforests and farms. In the south, in green temperate Tasmania, almost all the rivers are permanent. Situated in the rainy Roaring Forties, and with enough high country and mountains to snag the rain-laden clouds, Tasmania's annual rainfall challenges that of North Queensland.

The west, lacking an equivalent range of mountains, is dryer, although the south-west is well-watered, and the monsoonal north of Australia is very wet indeed for half the year. Rivers in the Kimberleys in Western Australia, and the huge East Alligator, Katherine and Daly Rivers rise to spectacular heights in the Wet, especially when confined in rocky gorges.

Many of Australia's most beautiful and spectacular waterfalls are to be found in national parks: Kakadu's Twin Falls and Jim Jim Falls, though commonly seen in the Dry, must be awe-inspiring in the Wet; Wallaman Falls, the second highest sheer drop in Australia is one of many in the Herbert River catchment which also boasts the lovely Millstream Falls; Serpentine Falls south of Perth or the Fitzroy Falls in the high sandstone cliffs of Moreton National Park are equally fascinating. Almost any national park in Tasmania is likely to have lovely falls, and within Cradle Mountain-Lake St Clair, Wild Rivers and the South West National Parks, are some of the most spectacular rivers and lakes in Australia.

Oddly enough, the lakes in this dry land come in a surprising variety of sizes and forms: shallow coastal lakes and marshes; the crater lakes of Mt Gambier, Tower Hill and the Atherton Tableland; the tarns and small glacial lakes of the Tasmanian highlands; and the calm beauty of the big 'traditional' lakes like Pedder and St Clair. Lake Pedder today is artificially large due to the damming and consequent flooding of the original lake. Much controversy surrounded this, because of the loss of some true wilderness country and a beautiful little lake. Conservationists also battled, this time successfully, to save the Franklin and Gordon Rivers which were threatened with damming to satisfy the government's hunger for more and more hydro-electric power. Fortunately for the rest of us, Tasmania's rivers and lakes are safe... for now.

River jetty, Kuranda, Queensland

118

Warrnambool, western Victoria

River estuary, Flinders Island

Kiewa River, Harrietville, north-east Victoria

Derwent River, Tasmania

Ovens River, Bright, north-east Victoria

Russell Falls, southern Tasmania

Hogarth Falls, Strahan, south-west Tasmania

Mountfield National Park, southern Tasmania

Floods, Mackay, Queensland

Ox-bow lakes, Mackay, Queensland

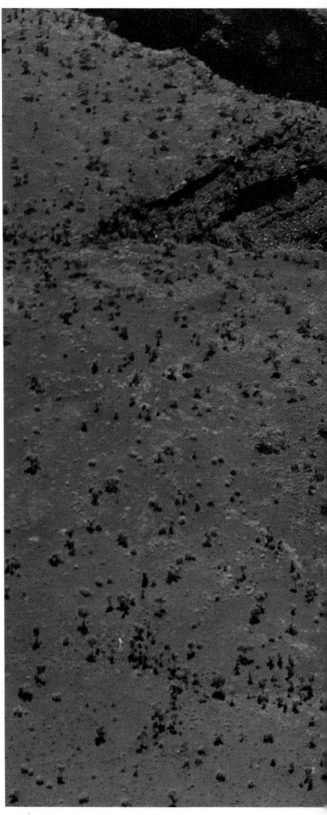

Outback river gorge, Northern Territory

Blue Lake, Mt. Gambier, South Australia

Mt. Murchison Lake, southern Tasmania

Mitchell River, Cairns, Queensland

Acknowledgements

First published in Australia in 1990 by:

Peter Antill-Rose and Associates
8/10 Anella Avenue
Castle Hill
New South Wales 2154
Australia

Copyright© Peter Antill-Rose and Associates

Photographs copyright© Gary Lewis

Photographs by Gary Lewis
Pictorial editing by Allan Cornwell

Designed by Small Back Room Productions, Upwey, Victoria
Typeset by Paragraphics, Ferntree Gully, Victoria
Produced in Hong Kong by Mandarin Offset

ISBN 1 86282 040 6

Roadsign, Northern Territory